DEDICATION

For lovers of that other realm, the place where all inspiration
emanates.

PRAISE FOR IN THE REALM OF SPIRIT

"In the Realm of Spirit: Psalms from a Mountain is prose poetry at its strongest, but does not always appear in the stanza format that is usual for poetic efforts. The result is often 'somewhere in between', a state of journeying described in a prose poem of the same name: *"Somewhere between the fork in the road and the narrow, overgrown path lies the way to the true destination..."*

Poetry enthusiasts not wedded to the idea that verse need be measured and fit into a given format will relish John A. Brennan's diverse collection for its flowing, descriptive language of personal, cultural and physical journeys and for its metaphors and meaning. This is not to say that such a form doesn't exist, here: prose poems are interspersed with thought-provoking passages that represent a strong poetic heartbeat: *"The stone-cold slab bruised hungry bones,/ as he lay on the floor all alone./ His life ebbed nigh, but his spirit held high,/ as soon he would feast with his own."*

His language strikes at the heart of mountains, men, and evolutionary processes of transformation, offering perspectives that are at once rooted in villages, mountains, and the rugged terrain of hearts and minds.

What evolves is an observational journey that follows mountains, valleys, and spiritual reflection alike: one that takes a progressive, haunting perspective as it traverses the hills and dales of an ancient land in search of those nuggets of enlightenment that stem from both a dispassionate observer and a nomad: *"I've been down in the green valley, the holy place; the place where pagan and saint walk the blessed earth yet still, in silent mystic. The one where the river flows ever onward to its birthplace, carrying the tortured history, winding slow with measured precision, to cast upon the ocean."*

Diane Donovan
Midwest Literary Services

Items should be returned on or before the date shown below. Items
not already requested by other borrowers may be renewed in person,
in writing or by telephone. To renew, please quote the number on the
barcode label. To renew online a PIN is required. This can be requested
at your local library.
Renew online @ **www.dublincitypubliclibraries.ie**
Fines charged for overdue items will include postage incurred in recovery.
Damage to or loss of items will be charged to the borrower.

Leabharlanna Poiblí Chathair Bhaile Átha Cliath
Dublin City Public Libraries

Comhairle Cathrach
Bhaile Átha Cliath
Dublin City Council

Marino Branch
Brainse Marino
Tel: 8336297

Due Date	Due Date	Due Date

New York, NY

Leabharlanna Poiblí Chathair Baile Átha Cliath

Dublin City Public Libraries

ISBN: 1722290641
ISBN-13: 978-1722290641
Library of Congress Control Number: 2018950284

ACKNOWLEDGEMENTS

This collection is dedicated to my peers and sources of continuing inspiration: Yeats, Shaw, O'Casey, Wilde, Joyce, Heaney etc. and is an acknowledgement of all seekers of peace and tranquility in the seen and unseen worlds.

A sincere thank you to Hofstra University and their stellar writing programs for enabling me to explore and develop my dormant skills; The Long Island Writers Guild, whose president Dennis T. Kotch and his wife Beverley always supported my efforts, and to John Walsh and the Irish Cultural Society of Garden City for their stellar efforts in keeping the spirit of both the written and spoken word alive.

And finally to the Irish American Writers and Artists in New York, I would like to express my heartfelt thanks for granting to me and so many artists the opportunity to share our work with the public.

FOREWORD

The man sitting in the back row of the meeting room had an uncommon brogue, not the Galway or Clare brogues of my family. Could he be a "left-footer" like our young speaker, a novelist from Northern Ireland? That man with the Armagh brogue was, we discovered, the man who took the road less traveled—and, Oh what a difference John A. Brennan has made for us in the Irish Cultural Society of Long Island. John was for us a "keeper."

We found that John Brennan's intimacy with the fourth, fifth and sixth centuries of Irish history helped him to create a refreshingly ancient ambiance at his talks at our meetings. He made Irish history our history; his "we," "us," and "our" were his usual pronouns, reminding us that we share the history and stories of his talk. We left his meetings as more Irish, proud that we shared St. Patrick, the Irish monks of Iona, and Cuchulain and other mythic heroes with the Irish from the "Old Country." As a writer, John's natural poetic style uses indirection to great effect. He entices the readers of his essay "The Master" published in the newsletter of the Irish Cultural Society to infer that the master was St. Patrick. His style in *In The Realm of Spirit* also challenges his readers not just to read but to engage with the poems. John the poet invites not right or wrong answers but rather promotes engagement with his art.

The dreamer is, indeed, John Brennan who refuses to die with regrets. He proved to the nay saying "boyos" who told him he would never pass the tests to become a custodial engineer that John Brennan is a yea sayer. He proved to himself that a working class Irishman could publish five books and win awards while doing so. He proved that grit and determination are wonderful complements to intelligence. He proved that the Irish can still produce heroes of resilience in today's world.

John Brennan did not have to study the parallelism, alliteration, and the rhythm which add pace and depth to his prose poems. The power of poetry comes naturally to a man from ancient Ireland who has steeped himself in Ireland's myths and legends. I like to think that it is probable that John fought in the Battle of Cúl Dreimhne to claim ownership of a book; doesn't the Irish literary tradition suggest that the Irish will wage war over books? It is likely, too, that John was the monk who was saved from the Loch Ness monster by St. Columcille; didn't most of the Irish saints earn their sainthood by rescuing Irish poets?

John A. Brennan brings the magic and melody of poetic inspiration to the world. Enjoy the experience.

John Walsh, Editor, Irish Cultural Society

PROLOGUE

Somewhere between the fork in the road and the narrow, overgrown path lies the way to the true destination, between the cold steel rail and the riverbank, hidden from weary eyes, it waits for you in patient silence. Somewhere between the fitful dream and the fright of morning reality the solution is within your grasp, between the cool forest and the field of dreams it hides in plain sight. Somewhere between the fiery crucible and the altar of salvation you confess and beg for forgiveness, between the moss-covered rock and the hard, unforgiving place of desperation it sits and calls on you to find it before it's too late. Somewhere between the frozen floes and the dry desert sands it begs you to look closer, between the lines the secret awaits discovery and offers you peace. Somewhere between the canyon floor and the lofty mountain top the pure air invites you to breathe, between the ocean depths and the edge of the universe new life beckons. Somewhere between the rainbow and the furthest reaches of the cosmos, it circles endlessly, between the whipping post and the hangman's pole you will bleed and absorb the pain. Somewhere between the womb and the final resting place you will be re-born.

John

CONTENTS

In The Realm of
Spirit
Psalms From A Mountain

JOHN A. BRENNAN

JOHN A. BRENNAN

Slieve Gullion in County Armagh

Birth of Gullion

They call me Gullion, mountain of steep slopes. I am old, old as time itself; older than the dawn of life, forged in the crucible of a ring of fire, before mankind existed. Up here the air is pure and fresh and crisp as the frost of winter's breath. I've seen it all from up here, here by the bottomless lake, here beside the elevated cairns and high burial places. Born of violent upheaval when the vast ice sheets melted, and the land was empty and free. Born before the outsiders came and changed it all with ignorant chaos and vicious perfidy. Nomads hunted and gathered on my slopes before the plains were cleared and the first crops planted.

I see it all from up here.

Tilting

Back then Plato drilled me, showed me, pushed me, cajoled me,
but I in my throes always knew better and rushed blindly, headlong,
driven by the heady arrogance of youth, toward my blurred,
unreachable horizon, desperate to climb the mountain, eager to rend
the curtain, cut the traces, burn the bridges, kick the door down,
grasp at straws, not knowing then that you can't always get what you
want, not realizing then that I didn't know what I wanted, with the
mentality of the lemming, breaking on through to the other side, a
savage savant, heedless, arrogant and lost. And all the while, in the
not-knowing, in that blissful ignorance, seeking enlightenment,
craving redemption, searching for solace, begging for forgiveness and
pleading for mercy, all the while not realizing that it was there within
all the time.

Into the Unknown

On a cold, wet, shrouded dawn, they bade farewell to their brothers and sisters and made their way down the cragged headland, to the shoreline, where dark, white capped waves, swept ashore by a fearsome gale, crashed angrily at their feet. Rain, relentless in harsh velocity, whipped about their bodies and stung their frightened faces with cold, cruel ferocity. Looking as one toward the Master, their eyes searched his face for answers, then watched as he climbed, surefooted, to the top of a flat, lichen covered rock. As he stood facing the ocean, he raised his arms toward the frightening sky. In his right hand, grasped firmly, was his old, oft used staff, the symbol of his otherworldly power. Standing there, with his windswept hair streaming around his broad face, his long cloak billowing like a sail unfurled, he began to chant. Softly at first, his voice soon soared upward and became louder than the very wind itself. In that instant, the clouds dispersed, and the water became a flat, blue, welcoming expanse. The Sun's rays, in their brilliance, warmed and dried them and they began to smile in the knowledge that all would be well. They were grateful to him for his guidance and strength, as he saved them once again. Then, with no fear, they cast off into the open sea, tacked west, and sailed out
into the unknown.

The Dreamer

Intoxicated with unbridled madness, a dreamer returned from a
pilgrimage, a sojourn, high in the Mourne mountains. Back to
reality, back to his brother and their bicycle shop. Back to his small,
unremarkable village in the valley. This dreamer had made the
pilgrimage many times before; had basked in the ever-present
silence, had given his thoughts free rein, let them soar. The crisp
bracken snapping underfoot, the fresh wind buffeting his face,
invigorated and filled him with optimistic fervor. He felt as one
with the mountains, the sky and the cosmos. But this time
something was different, he was different, he had changed. Giddy
and lightheaded he wondered, just for an instant,
am I going mad?
Strolling through the 'silent valley,' he rested near a patch of gorse,
the yellow blooms vibrant in the afternoon sun. Eyes turned
upward and scanned the cloudless sky. Marveled as two hawks
wheeled and circled high above, wide-spread wings in silhouette
against the sharp blueness. *If only I could do that.* On down, down
through a thick carpet of heather, in the distance, the small lime-
washed cottage.
A row of new bicycles lined up outside the shop. Watched the
sunlight glinting off the frames. Watched his brother, leaning over
the stone bridge, gazing at the flowing stream beneath. *I wonder what
he's thinking?* The dreamer's mind took him on a fantastical flight of
fancy, transported him to a far-off land, a land across the wild, grey
Atlantic Ocean. Thought of two other brothers and a place called
Kitty Hawk, in that moment, right then, right there, in that place,
the dreamer knew
he had to fly.

Lough Ross at Sunset

Early morning by the Lough

A serene aura enveloped the Lough that morning.
Air, pure and frigid, sharp on intake, rustled the leaves in the
hedgerow that ran to the water's edge and sent a Goldfinch
skyward. Traces of wispy, low-lying mist, just above the surface,
slowly evaporated as the first rays of sunlight crept over the
landscape, bathing all in a glorious,
glimmering glow.
A lone Hare, fearful eyes wide, drank from a rock-pool, and
bounded back up the hill to safety. A pair of mute Swans, white
and majestic, paired for life, sailed silently toward their nest among
the reeds and rushes, content and free. A small flock of newly
shorn sheep grazed quietly on the still shaded, dew covered, grassy
slopes in the distance.
The water, a flat mirrored expanse, stretched in all directions, out
from the black rock. In reflection, a small, tree-covered island,
aimlessly, endlessly floating, on blue crystal water. A boat, the lone
rower, pulling with easy, practiced strokes, caused widening,
hurried ripples to race toward the far shore. A loud splash startled
as a prowling Pike leapt from the depths,
eager for breakfast.
Sights and sounds of an early, shimmering morning on the shores
of Lough Ross. The ancient trees guarding the rath, high on Corliss
hill, watch all below with quiet resolve, ever mindful of the
whispers of men long gone, and their enduring
plans for freedom.

Sojourn

Fatigue tells us that it is time to fill our lantern, grasp our staff and
sojourn in the forest. There, beside the cool stream that flows ever
onward, we sit at the mouth of the cave and begin the inner work.
Fear not the dappled fawns as they eye with
loving intent, nor the goldfinch as he warbles his message from
atop the purple thistles.

The woods will be bright and resound with the serenity of oneness.

Though ribs may be cracked, and flesh may be torn, and nails may
be old rusted spikes. Thorns driven deep, and flail ripped flesh all
make for a terrible sight. But a beauty is born of the sufferance,
once the path through the woods it is trod.
With lantern bright and staff held tight, we resurrect and emerge
with our God.

The Meadow Ballet

Say what you like about my old man, but he could handle a scythe. Could swing it with the easy grace of a matador in a bullring in Barcelona. Could turn and pivot, sure of foot, like a lithe ballerina on the stage at the Bolshoi.

The grass, defeated with surgical precision, fell in complete surrender prostrate beneath him, each cut a perfect arc of knowing the way. He would spit on his palms, grasp the handles surely, but lightly.

Glints of sunlight would flash like mirrored signals with each slice. The steel, sharp as obsidian, mowed with near silent swish.

Wielded like a gladius before the barbaric grasses, he made the meadowlark and linnet flee in frightful flight before him, feathers ruffled. The field-mice scurried helter-skelter, squealing for mercy. And always at full stretch, that graceful swing, that perfect step, the meadow ballet. The stone, couched in the back pocket, waited it's turn.

He would pause, straighten his back and stand the scythe on end, dulled blade pointed at the earth. Would wipe the sweat from his brow with the back of his hand, slide the stone along its length and up the other side. Hone with an angle of perfect degree, steady, sure. The reaper's shadow, long and black, lay outstretched on the stubble behind him. Would drink deeply from the can of milk, and then…

the second act.

The Singing Bones

Inside my father's bones lie a million secrets. Secrets passed down
the long chain from the beginning of time and the vastness of
space. In the glorious mix of diversity, endlessly
coursing through the shrouded mists of the Holy Island, he
breathes still. The memories of his people, absorbed by the stones
and the very earth herself, exhale all that ever was.
Their essence still permeates, insisting that it
be never forgotten.

From Cessair, through Fomorian, Partholonian, Nemedian, Fir
Bolg, Tuatha, Milesian, Celt, Saxon, Viking and Norman, I
inhaled that cocktail of life with eager lungs and magnificent
surprise. I am inside my father's bones and my father is inside
mine. He is the beggar-man, the holy man, the master and the
freeman. He still walks the fields, sure of foot. He still wades the
stream, fearless. He still lures the trout, with quiet assuredness. He
still charms the goldfinch from her tree-top perch,
ever gently.

His bones sing loud enough for me to hear
even in the darkest, deepest reaches of the
night. On a quiet evening, I still hear his melodic
whistle floating on the air, calling to me. Yes, I
am inside my father's bones,
and he is inside mine.

The Solstice

From the stone of Fal on Tara high, 'cross the river that flows deep and slow, the ancients all gather at this holy place to catch the bright morning's warm glow. In robes of pure white, they walk the ground and wait for the rising sun. In the heart of the mound, old souls can be found; heaven bound, they now become one. The Master appears, an unearthly sight, and raises his arms to the sky. The people bow down, and kneel on the ground, then chant with a joyful cry. The rays creep across the hills and the glen, and strike the box over the door. They follow along to the chamber, and then, the love there enshrined, proudly soars. It has always been done in this very way, and for eons will last evermore. Their spirits will rise and fly every day, and watch over our true heart's core.

The Green Valley

I've been down in the green valley, the holy place; the place where pagan and saint walk the blessed earth yet still, in silent mystic. The one where the river flows ever onward to its birthplace, carrying the tortured history, winding slow with measured precision, to cast upon the ocean.

Down where the sacred hills, those silent sentinels to the glorious, tragic past, keep watch in painful solitude. Down where the spirits keen and await each dawn with hopeful intent of peaceful morn. Down where the lonesome, royal fort is no more, the ramparts trampled roughshod and buried underfoot. Down where memories of olden kingly splendor died 'neath the invaders harsh heel. Down where the royal plain stretches, forlornly grasping at the distant, unreachable horizon.

Down where the stone of destiny sits in erect remembrance, remembering. Where ancient Brehons, in their yellow robes, inscribed the laws of the common man in flowing ogham script. Where the magicians cast the spells of the Tuatha and conjured up the Fianna, the young ones, the ones who would fight to save them.

Down where the sacred mound inhales the essence of all that has gone before, and exhales all that will ever be, the inscribed stones ever alive. Down where the sun aligns in glorious magnitude within the cloistered, chambered walls. Down where the haunting, haunted battle cries beseech the blooded banks and echoes among the reeds and rushes.

Down where the lark soars straight as a fletchers' creation, upward, up to the blue heaven, and sings. Down where the final slaughter reached it's bloody, brutish, end on the wide plains of royal Midhe;

the old King gone, the planted pretender crowned with a foreign, alien hand, the scepter cursed.

Down where the blood-soaked shields, awash in the churning torrent, sailed out upon the reddened river. Down where the fields absorbed the crimson life force of the vanquished, grotesquely strewn, dead, in furrow, bracken and tussock.

The Hill

On Tara's sacred hill are found,
in unison and heartfelt troth.
A pair of old true lovers bound,
by brehon law and Celtic knot.
The spirits gather all around,
with their power they now instill.
In moonbeam bright and clear starlight,
two claddagh rings fulfill.

He holds her to his beating heart,
and swears his love this night.
The maid she swears they'll never part,
evermore will their souls take flight.
They walk across the valley floor,
to the mound above the Boyne.
And offer there to ancient yore,
their souls and hearts and minds.

A saddled mare for them awaits,
in patient silence and to greet.
This pair who here have coupled fate,
together now, night bound and fleet.

Valleys and Dust

I've been down in the old valley, *his* valley, the secret one. The one
where blown sand slices like slivers of obsidian. Where silent
passages wind and curl into an underworld of immortals, hidden,
sealed forever in canopic jars. Eternity whispers aloud from hewn
stones telling of our future and their past. Mortals in bleached
white shrouds of linen, wound, wrapped, arms crossed, old bones
strewn, forgotten, again and again. Still, always the jackal, watching,
seeing. In his jaundiced eye, reflections of re-birth concealed, then
revealed like second skin, dry and stiff, like parchment.
I've been down in her valley too. She with the piercing eyes and the
false beard, ruling in lieu, serene and wise with immortal beauty;
carriage and mien royal, deified, the flail across the crooked staff.
And always Anubis, watching, protecting forgotten spaces. I've
been down in Sheba's vale, now sundered and awash in a false sea.
He, greatest son of Ra, moved, taken, swamped with man's desire
and vulgar greed. The cavern silent, awaits and beckons the return.
Glyphs scored deep in pylon and obelisk rise up, up greeting Ra,
the holy one, the anointed. With feather and hearts' ultimate test,
Isis awaits in patient silence. Osiris ever present, inviting to home,
across the vast divide.

Canyons and Dust

I've been down in the sacred canyon. The one where the spirits
keen aloud in the dark. Down where red dust swirls in the hot, dry
wind with incessant, insistent erosion. Down where the parched
wadis beseech the heavens for water, the pueblos, sad, scorched
remnants. The one where, in ages past, the Clovis peoples wove
their storage baskets. Down where the hand-hewn rock shelters
bear witness to a dead existence, the enigmatic messages visible on
the bare walls, a stark reminder. The pit houses gone, the kivas
sundered, making way for the next brave tribes to
dwell.

Down where the stone blocks age and shimmer in the relentless
heat, a silent testament to the once great Anasazi, the ancient ones.
Down where dry, brittled shards glint amid the junipers and
lonesome canyon walls, baking in the scorched sand. Down where
the coyote wails at night, longing, his forlorn cries echoing, lost in
his mourning. Down where dense, shading forests once flourished,
green and majestic. All gone now. dust in the harsh, unforgiving
wind.

Yet, if it is quiet and still and if the sun is still above the horizon,
and if you are tuned to the other realm, you will absorb their
presence as you walk among and marvel at what remains of their
once, multi-level dwellings. All laid out in perfect symmetry and a
mirror image of the Cosmos. A testament to their skillful hands
and brilliant minds.

The stones, cut with exquisite detail and built with such
mathematical and astronomical precision, defy all understanding.
You will be as one with the Great Spirit as the natural mystical
energy, afloat on the air, tangible in its permeation, invades your
senses, envelops you utterly and slowly draws you in, inviting you
in to their world, a world long gone, across and beyond the
vastness of space and time.

Legends and Heroes

Up here, before the blood of battle stained my soul, Foinn, cursed by the hag, swam in my lake. His people, the Fianna, protected my slopes. Here, Cullan the blacksmith named me and built his house from my rugged rocks and stones. Up here Setanta met the king, killed the hound and was re-named by the druid Cathbhadh. From my peak, the warrior watched the army of Maeve advance from the west, cross the open plain and push through the north gap, the sunlight glinting off their weapons. He lay in wait, then struck them down with ferocious intent, and saved the red bull of Cooley.
I see it all from up here.

Avenues and Dust

I've been down in the swamp valley, the place of reeds, birthplace
of the Gods. The one where the eagle grasped the serpent in its'
taloned grip atop the flowering cactus. The one where the
frightened refugees sought shelter, their old lands dead from
violent, volcanic upheaval, forcing them to flee and be reborn in
new hope of light.
Down where the chinampas, the raised beds, tamed the stagnant
swamps and life began anew, blessed and
fruitful.

Where the water channels, dug deep, made travel by canoe
possible. Down where the absence of fortification attested to the
peaceful Utopia and selective cultural diffusion. Down where thin
orange pottery and exquisitely crafted obsidian tools, honed by
ancient hands, were sent out and utilized widely among all of the
peoples. Down where echoes of Totonac, Olmec, Toltec, Zapotec,
Mixtec, Maya and Aztec blend and infuse with poignant
permeation.

Down where urbanism took hold defiantly, and proudly
proclaimed its existence. Down where the avenue stretches past
talud styled pyramids of Sun and Moon and the temples reach to
the heavens. Down where the feathered serpent rose skyward and
soared in magnificent
glory.

The Storm

We were expecting her unwelcome visit thanks to the ingenious
invention of Radar, which had been developed during the dark,
frightful years of World War II. All we could do was prepare for
her inevitable onslaught. She was conceived and born on the
African continent and like all newly born, was small, but would
soon grow into an uncontrollable,
raging demon.

She knew that she would be well fed as she wafted slowly out over
the rugged coastline and started her journey of utter destruction. She
met several others just like herself as she travelled westward, all from
the same nursery. Soon, they joined together in their deadly dance
and began their feeding frenzy. The ocean temperature being warmer
than normal became a vast, sustaining hotplate and she delighted
in this.

The suction created by her rotating winds allowed her to draw
copious amounts of moisture into her ravenous coils and
encouraged her to spin furiously. As she approached the Leeward
Islands she knew that a useless name and meaningless numbers
would be assigned to her in a futile attempt to understand her.
Maybe it was believed that in doing so it might lessen her fury, but
she knew better. She had become a grotesque, howling monster
and desired to enter the
history books.

She was the first of many, many more to come and now there
would be no stopping her. Sated, she headed straight for the
nearest land mass to wreak
her vengeance.

The Enchantress

They used to say she was different, and not of their world, this
strange woman of the forest. She spoke gently to the animals and
they responded with affection. Of earthly treasure, she cared not a
whit. Always in commune with her surroundings, she walked her
chosen, winding pathway with assured
steps.

At the stream in the glow of an early moon, she disrobed and
immersed in the cool, healing waters. As the water caressed and
washed over her, she shivered and thought of the Masters' touch.
Her body, now in its primal state of openness, her tongue tingled
with that familiar sense of desire. As she submerged, her wild, dark
mane floating on the surface, glistened in the soft
light.

Fawns, gathered along the banks to watch and protect, reflected
her image in their large, sloe shaped eyes. When she stepped out of
the waters, she spread her arms, threw her head back, and with the
moon rays caressing her, she sang. Low voiced at first, her sound
became louder and soon soared upward on the night air.
She had become the
Enchantress.

Gathering the leaves and herbs from the trees and bushes, she
anointed her body with their scented juices. She was ready to go to
him knowing he would be waiting. He was all that she desired. He
was prepared to die for her love. Their union had been blessed by
the learned men on the sacred hill, and now, their marriage would
be completed on this night,
in the forest.

She

Within the written she resides in quiet assurance of her place. Lithe
and languid, with regal mien, she glides from the page bearing gifts.
The mantle, flowing through the ages, envelops her in verity
profound. Gently musing all the while, in soft tones of measure,
knowing. The voice, breath soft in sublime caress, whispers, it's all
good and good as so ever sought, sighs. Her fair abstraction,
niched in careful frame, illuminates the recess where the wayward
seeker dwells. The essence of comfort, awaits its release from
restraint of time, space and ethereal sublimity. The sweet words
roll on.

Consider

Consider yourself truly blessed if one day you are allowed the immaculate gift of stroking the silken fur of a tiny, strangely unafraid, blind shrew, as she patiently gathers one by one, a selection of nuts and seeds left out for the backyard creatures. Consider yourself further blessed if the same gift is offered you by a frantic chipmunk as she feeds voraciously and stuffs her face pouch to capacity, hell bent on stocking up for the coming winter. Consider yourself in tune with the other realm if a young blue jay, with it's not yet developed head dress and unusually quiet for a change, flits and lands on your armrest, then drops a feather in your lap.

Did these small creatures sense that my troubled mind was fighting to understand and make sense of the horrific events happening in our world today? Did they seek to console me and assure me that there is indeed another realm, a place of quiet sanctuary? Did that new mother squirrel bring her three newly weaned babies to see me as a sign for humanity? To sit with me for a long while to tell me that despite the nightmarish happenings around and upon a convulsing mother earth, despite all of this, there is hope?

Were they sent to assure me that notwithstanding the absence of sanity and rational thought among those supposed to protect and lead us and the seeming reversal of all that is good and kind, despite it all, are they telling me that we as a race will survive, or are they telling me that if we don't return to our original nature we will have no choice but to start over again from the beginning?

We are a deeply flawed species, banished long age for committing the exact same acts of wanton negativity and disregard for all, that we still commit today. We are supposed to slowly evolve and become better with the passing of time, but in fact we are regressing. We have learned nothing and have invented a thousand religions to assure ourselves of our importance and bolster our voracious ego. We have ignored the core truth that we are here to advance civilization, not destroy it. Maybe it's time we went back and sat a while longer in the garden and take a good long look around.

The Swans

He glides across the smooth lakes' surface, but she is nowhere in sight. Stately he moves on ever through the night. A moonbeam beckons to a hidden place where once they did dwell. Faster now, maybe she lays there, and love again might they share. But no earthly sign now,
only pain.

Mute, and no sound escapes. The reeds and rushes lay empty. The archer with arrows more plenty, has struck in her hearts' place. He follows the fading silver beam upward, up toward the eternal light.

The lake is quiet now, now that the swans have gone. Once they sailed its wide surface, silent and free. A ghostly presence is all that lingers on, to remind us of what there used to be. He searched for her, but alas, no trace, no sight. Meshed together now, mid the moons' clear light. His last song silent sung, from deep within. Then, merging slowly with the mist,
he fades from without.

The Rapparee

He rode from high to the valley floor,
and hid behind the old Rowan tree.
It was time to settle a deep-set score
and seek vengeance for his family.

They took the land, they took their pride,
rode roughshod o'er the scattered bones.
With mace and mail from far and wide,
castles shook, to the bare keep stones.

But now 'midst leaves, and masked and
still, flintlock and cutlass tried and true.
A glossy mare to do his will those in
league, are now sure to rue.

Coach rims crunch on graveled base
two pairs snort, wild manes aquiver.
He spurs her on, now quick apace.
"Halt there coachman, stand and deliver!"

Mars Bars and Scars

Dreaming of the planet Mars, wistfully thinking upon fallen stars.
We found ourselves behind prison bars, me and Jesus, showing our
scars and remembering the magical nights in those wild Irish bars.
Searching for paradise, our souls on ice, choosing virtue over vice.
We remake the divine sacrifice by being all too human, me and
Molloy.

Traveling through time and space seeking the original universe, and
finding a sacred place to sing of the blessings and to nurse the
curse.

See how to be. Let the light set you free,eternal now, shining into
the black and blue void on this good, godly night. Live and let live
is all there is, the road less traveled he chose, having no choice. To
become the ultimate sacrifice for
me and Molloy.

The Castle

She walks the crumbling walls in dead of night and casts a dead eye
on the hinterland. To the north, the wide gap and the old road-way
from Tara, still wending its way to Macha. The stones ever alive
beneath her feet, the moat long dried up, reminds of glory days
past. Knights horse hoofs once rang on the cobbled courtyard
below, returning from battlefields. The keep, where the plunder
taken from the chieftains and holy men lay safe, now wasted.

Hidden passages trod in secret by both lovers and priests, are silent
testament to all before. The saint's well that slaked the thirst of all
within the bounds, dry and empty, echoes forlorn. The tower, door
high above the ground, a sanctuary, sits mute and waits in quiet
solitude. Winding stairs, the treads worn by footsteps of ten
thousand mortals, now in desolation. The window, where her
husband fell, reveals its painful memory of cold, cruel murder.

And so Rohesia walks, her search never ends, seeking peace, where
no peace can ever exist.

Going Home

They brought Eilidh home today, home across the sea to her
beloved island. Home to rest among her people, among the rocks
and soil of the remote, windswept Outer Hebrides. A little Celtic
girl, with a love of music, now led home by the lone piper playing
her favorite slow airs.
In her casket, draped in the green and white flag of Barra, Eilidh
lies still and at peace with the universe. As the small plane landed,
her parents on board, family and friends waited on the strand,
tearful, hearts broken.
Firemen, friends and locals carried her remains at waist height,
across the sand to the waiting hearse. Eilidh is home now, home at
last, welcomed by the swirl of the pipes, home at last, among her
people, home at last in the heart of
the Western Isles.

Alone

The stone-cold slab bruised hungry bones,
as he lay on the floor all alone.
His life ebbed nigh, but his spirit held high,
as soon he would feast with his own.
The visions he saw, the hope that he felt,
would never be taken by force.
His will was complete, his heart, one last beat,
now the way, he would lead to the source.
Asking, "Why, oh why did you have to die
on this accursed foreigner's floor?"
Saying, "It has to be me, so it will not be you,
Now, I'll go and throw open the door."
The piper's lament is heard in wide space,
as the warrior was laid in his grave.
The lark soared high in a sorrowful sky,
as he left us to join with the brave.

Ellen

"She is not dead, she doth sleep.
'tis death is dead; weep not for Her."

Sure, God help them, the poor crathurs," was her oft used
expression.
Ellen was a simple woman, happiest when surrounded by those less
fortunate, the 'different' ones, the afflicted, the children and the
strays. And they all migrated to her doorstep. They sought her out,
as if they knew she could and would save them. As if they were
sent to her. As if they were guided by a loving, unseen hand, to her
door. As if they knew that she would understand them. They could
see her bright candle, always alight in her window, even on the
darkest deepest nights. And they basked in her lightness and they
loved her and told her so. Her love for others was of the unspoken
kind. The kind that comes from somewhere unearthly. The kind
that endures through the vastness of time, space and beyond. A
serene aura surrounded her always and when she spoke it was in
the softest tones of measure.
"Come on in and sit down. I'll put on the kettle and we'll have a
wee cup of tea."
Weep not for her, for she doth sleep, 'tis death is dead.

The Poet's Glen

I slept, as a boy in the Poet's Glen, beneath the red hand and a starlit, south Armagh sky, content and free. The river, flowing with measure of precise destination, lulled with quiet cascade. Olden, mossed oaks and elms, branched wide and reached for the essence of the ever-present Bard.

O'Neill, asleep in the churchyard vault, amused, listened to the nocturnal chorus and smiled. I dreamed of McCooey, MacAliondain and the outlaw MacMurphy, together forever, locked in immortal embrace. Still, in quiet unison, they sing the praise of the Lord of the Fews.

In the distance, above the lake, the castle beckoned them all, pleaded their return to home. A young moon bathed the pasture, the trees, the church and river with silvery light and a lone blackbird sang her lament, forlorn, in the cool night air of Creggan vale.

In the early light of dawn, a morning stroll along the trail of the poets, past the gardens, past the Church and the Great house, brought to mind, thoughts of heroes past and present. The graveyard guards its secrets well, with tenacious grasp, for revelation in future time. Yet ever still, the salmon will run and leap over the rocky waterfall under the bridge, bringing the eternal knowledge home once more.

The Slaughter

Sated, the invaders retreated; in their wake, a bare, devastated wasteland as far as the horizon. Smoke from still smoldering fires in the fields and storehouses hung heavy on the air, choking and stinging the eyes of the few remaining survivors. Butchered corpses of both human and animal lay strewn in grotesque indifference where they fell, the royal enclosure breached, sacked, burned, and left in ruin.

The headless corpses of the nobles, mutilated in a frenzied orgy of bloodlust, silenced; the royal lifeforce seeping into the earth. The church and monastery, which once sang the praises of both king and creator, reduced to piles of scorched, scattered stones, forlorn.

The houses, usually filled with love, laughter and joyous celebration, razed with violent hatred, a pitiful sight. Everything of value, including surviving livestock, religious artifacts and the women and children, were dragged to the ships for transport.

Rambling

Rambling is good for the soul: it brings us back to the time when
we all were nomads, with no constraints, and in the soft, warm,
misty Irish rain it is a wonderful, almost spiritual experience. There
is a sense of freedom that's truly intoxicating. I went rambling most
days after school and looked forward to the weekends. The secret
was to get off the road as soon as possible and as I knew where all
the openings in the hedges and the gaps in the walls were, I could
be in that other wild, parallel world of nature in
minutes.

The smell of wet heather wafts and mingles with the sweet aroma
of the open countryside and the stillness seems to envelop all. I
would pause and listen for the caws of the crows atop the branches
of a sprawling oak tree or the melodic song of a goldfinch as he
called his mate from a patch of thistles. Sometimes, a startled
rabbit, scared by a wily fox, would dart out from beneath a tangle
of gorse bushes, his large brown eyes wide with fear as he ran for
safety. Off in the distance the faint lowing of grazing cows could
be heard if I stopped and was perfectly still. Then the quiet would
descend again, dropping
slowly.

Oliver

Beneath the tree near Oswulf's stone, where the roman roads met the river, a blood-soaked spot and a hangman's knot would soon a soul deliver. No guilt nor shame would mark the name of this man from the holy vale, tho' a king's command forced him to stand three miles from Newgate jail.

From proud Loughcrew in royal Midhe all the way to the apostle's ground his journey took him far and wide to help spread the word around. Brutal laws were passed to bind him fast to a foreign cruel hand but with cloak and veil and a well-worn trail, he fled north to Macha's land.

With Phelim the bard he found shelter and slept in in the minstrel's bed, while on Gullion's slopes roguish Titus Oates and his popish plot brought dread, to the Doctor's house in the valley, near the lime kilns at old Lislea, to Mullaghbawn and O'Hanlon's fort and Forkhill beyond Sturgan Brae.

The hunters followed his footsteps and sought after him night and morn for the bounty set and the fear of the threat that his words would lead and warn. From Charles and his vile henchmen and their masters in London town he shifted and shaped across field and wide lake and fooled both a king and his crown.

But up on the back of a horsecart with his arms and legs tightly bound the time was now come to stand and not run for escape would never be found. As the rope drew tight and took his light and the bright sun turned to grey, he offered it up in a martyr's cup and departed this world on that day.

The Smith

In a hellish crucible, amid an inferno of cascading, fiery sparks, he forged like Vulcan and his father before him. At his mercy, pigs of cold, dead iron came alive as the hammer fell in a ferocious arc of brutal creation. The anvil, solid and strong, sang loud with every blow as he fought the metal and beat it 'til it yielded to his skilled command. Clouds of billowing steam, spat, hissed and filled the air as he doused the white-hot metal in the vat of cold water, tempering to hard weapons of construct.

Bellows pumped, fire coked, flames flared bright and once more, the ceremony began anew.

The Impasse

Tortured with feelings of unease and worrisome thoughts, he began to have a frightening, recurring dream. In the dream, he was naked and tied to a large, white oak tree, the last one standing. The symbols of his birthright and power, his inscribed stones of divination and his oft-used staff, lay scattered and broken on the ground at his feet. All across the land the sacred oak groves had been cut down and burned on large pyres and the hilltop fortress was gone. In its place on the hill above the wide valley, he could see a high, wooden cross, silhouetted against the backdrop of the western sky. A strange man, holding a staff with a crooked top, appeared to be addressing a large crowd, was calling his name and with outstretched arms, beckoning him to join them. The dream worried him, and he knew that it was only a matter of time until it's deeper meaning became clear.

Incursions

From my summit, I watched Egfrid, the Saxon with his brutal armies, destroy, pillage and take my people as slaves to foreign lands. I wept as the Norsemen sailed into the place of the 'dark pool' to wreak their havoc and plunder and burn with merciless mindlessness. I stood helpless as the Normans conquered with frightening force and took my rocks to build their castles and great houses.

Up here, I listened to the bards when they met in the summer and announced the coming of the young Pretender, giving birth and free reign to words of hope that transcend the ages and still echo across the fields and valleys, carried on the wind. I cheered as the rapparee from Carnally outran the scourge of the Fews and made way to the safety of the hideout at Flagstaff.

I see it all from up here.

The Roman

Walking along, he let his mind wander, back to the fateful day when the wild, pagan marauders attacked his village and family home, burning and looting with impunity. He recalled his mother and father shouting at him and his sisters, urging them to run and hide and the fear and panic as the young men and girls, including him and his sisters, were rounded up and taken to the boats.

He remembered his time as a shepherd, tending to the sheep and goats on the rugged granite crags of the cold, wet mountain and the absolute loneliness surrounding him like a burial shroud, sustained only by his unwavering faith. He shivered as he thought of the stormy nights when the howling wind roared, and the thunder rocked the very ground where he lay trembling in abject fear.

He could still feel the crackle of electricity on his skin as he thought of the night sky ablaze with fiery light, the furze and bracken lit with an eerie, hellish glow, each flash etched in his memory forever. He recalled how he had prayed earnestly every day imploring God to free him from his bondage and allow him to return safely to his family.

By God's grace he had survived it all; intimidation, threats of imprisonment, death and banishment, but he was aware that there was still considerable opposition to him and his new message.

Dark Times

Back then war was the ever-present companion and the FBI and
the CIA and the IRA and the BBC and the fingerprint files
crowded and smothered the senses. Back then blood flowed
crimson down the streets of my town, congealed and then stained
the holy ground. Back then Bobby starved to death in Long Kesh
prison camp, his fingernails blackened. His body consumed from
within. Skeletal remains a stark reminder of nine more to follow his
lead, willing political pawns.

Back then Joe escaped to the sanctuary of Manhattan's upper
eastside, tended bar at Clancy's, until the canary sang his traitors
song. Back then Fergal was shot to death on a Sunday morning
after mass, another innocent slaughtered.

Back then one man one vote was still just a dream and the street
fighting men were on fire. The fighting men from Crossmaglen,
harried, hunted, revered. Pacifists turned into reluctant, universal
soldiers for the cause. Back then Sunday was bloodied in Derry,
thirteen their number. Gone. Immortals now. Back then the women
in Armagh Jail were violated, invaded and defiled. Back then,
innocence died.

Battle of the Book

On an open plain, two armies led by holy men, faced each other across the wide expanse and prepared to go to war over a book. Nothing could stop it, not even the intervention of respected Olamhs with cultured words of appeasement. The die was cast, life force would flow and stain the furrows and bracken as far as the horizon.
At day's end, three thousand lay dead and dying in mortal agony. Death throes, haunting, pitiful screams, resounding on the soft evening air, were heard on Tara, some miles distant. Blood-soaked shields and broken claidebs lay scattered all around, some still clasped in the hands of the butchered, broken bodies of the vanquished.

When it was over, the survivors left in their wake, a bare, devastated wasteland from horizon to horizon. Acrid smoke, from still smoldering fires in the fields hung heavy on the air. Headless corpses, both human and animal lay strewn in grotesque indifference where they fell, razed with violent hatred, a pitiful sight.

That night, a pall of deathly silence enveloped the sorrowful plain, nothing stirred for days. The holy men, clutching the books to their breasts, departed the scene and went home.

Crossing the Lake

The long drawn out whoop of a howler monkey shattered the
silence and echoed all around. As the echo faded the silence
dropped again, slowly. The stillness enveloping the lake that
morning was perfect. The air, pure and cold, could be tasted.
Traces of the wispy, low lying mist that hung just above the surface
were slowly evaporating as the sun climbed lazily in the
eastern sky.
The flatness of the lake was a mirrored expanse stretching away
from our canoe in all directions, and the reflection of a small, tree
covered Island floating aimlessly off in the distance was crystal
clear on the cold, azure water. A shimmering, pink skinned,
freshwater dolphin broke smoothly from the depths and seemed to
smile at us as it arched and slid gently
back under.

The Pagan King

The sole occupant of the Great Hall on that day was no ordinary mortal and anyone observing him would have been struck by his stature and regal mien. Long haired, full bearded and standing almost six feet tall, his long-sleeved tunic, fashioned by skilled weavers from gleaned flax plants, was colored bright red and reached down well below his knees.

A broad leather belt, circled his waist, held his wand of office, a dagger, a small pouch and helped keep his leine in place. His four folded, richly embroidered woolen cloak, had the five colors of the nobility, was trimmed with fox fur, reached almost to the floor and pinned with an ornate golden broach at his right shoulder.

Around his neck hung the gold chain of valor that he had inherited from his father, signifying his status as a warrior. His hand stitched sandals, tanned from the soft hide of a fallow deer were dyed purple, denoting his rank, wrapped around his ankles and were held together with strings of leather.

Shake up

Give Scotland back to the Irish and Wales to the Isle of Man, move England back to America, where all the trouble began. Spain would occupy Britain and France could stay where she is, if we move Africa over to China and India down to Cadiz. Send Belgium up to the Artic and Portugal across to Taiwan, sell Russia off to the Aussies and New Zealand goes to Japan.

Swap India with Alaska and ship Italy off to Peru, the Germans off to Siberia and Poland to Katmandu. The Greeks go to Mauritius and Morocco is given to Crete, Egyptians go to Israel and the new world is almost complete. Honduras now becomes Malta and Jamaica is now Pakistan, the Dutch to Outer Mongolia and Luxembourg moves to Siam.

Cuba goes to Hawaii, Samoa shifts to the Hebrides, Honduras is now called Sri Lanka, Norway is now Senegalese. The Aluetians drop down to Mauritius and Fiji absconds with Hunan, Korea is now called Alberta and Denmark is twinned with Oman. Manilla replaces Croatia, Baghdad is now Vietnam. Barbados now Guatemala and St. Lucia become Amsterdam.

The new world order is ready, it'll be completed at last, if we send all politicians to Hades and hop to it, speedy and fast.

Saints and Holy Men

From up here I watch over the ancient places, at rest down below my granite crags and gorse covered flanks. The 'churches of the mountain,' now empty and forlorn, cradle the saint in her earthly repose. Her holy well still flows, unstoppable, with quiet, fluid meander. From here I can see the ancient roadway that wends its way to Macha, the old fort.

I can see down in the valley, the 'crooked lake' where the people fished and swam. I can see both Cashel and Carrigan's loughs where the water is still pure and clear as crystal, ice cold to the taste. I watch over the 'church of the priests' and Ternoc's inscribed stone, still standing proud in majestic defiance on the old road from Tara.

I see it all from up here.

Martin

They carried him back today, the boy who became a man of the streets. Back to Derry, back through the streets in the sleet and the icy, March rain.

Back through the very same streets of childhood memory, the streets where the people cried out for equality, the streets where no man was equal. Streets where others ruled, and persisted in their archaic beliefs. Back through the streets that cried out for a savior, a fighter, a leader, a ray of hope in the dark night of soulless indifference. And he came, and he stood, and he fought and did what many of us did not have the courage to do.

Farewell Martin, your name joins the pantheon now.

The Silence

As he lay there in the after silence, bloody arms and legs scattered all around him, he thought of her and her large brown eyes. He thought of the old man in the corner, playing the fiddle. He thought of the river and the meadow where the lark soared, up toward the blue heaven. He thought of his father and the fishing rod. He thought of his pal Bobby and the magical times, he thought of the songs and the laughs. Then, with one last look around, he closed his eyes and surrendered the ghost.

The Flawed Mortal

An ill wind blew in off the Ocean, disturbed the arid, coarse white sand, swept through the open atria and courtyards, swirled around the painted columns and rustled the leaves on the olive trees in the garden belonging to the procurator. In a gilded chair, near to an open window, head bowed, brow furrowed, sat a troubled man, a man about to couple his fate for eternity, with another tortured soul...

Stumbling along a road strewn with crushed olive branches and anguished memories, a flawed mortal ran blindly toward the illusion of enlightenment. He ran, wearing a vagabond's shoes, the soles sewn and patched with empty gallows humor, guilt ridden sacrifice and self-slaughter. The overloaded corridors in his brain, an accumulation of sins of omission and disconnected ideals, cursed him, cursed his silent reproach and mocked his fluttering heart. Keeping only the photos that flattered and a carpet bag full of masks, he ran.

Behind him, an endless stream of hard-nosed, sickening sycophants, a parade of jeering jesters, a vanguard of withered mountebanks, a retinue of jaded dilettantes and a phalanx of pariahs and false prophets. On he ran, hounded by a mob of pitch-forked peasants baying for blood, with murder in their eyes. On he ran toward redemption and the sanctuary of resurrection, and as he ran, a raconteurs' label, hanging by a thread from his dusty, sweat stained coat, flapped wildly in the slipstream and followed him down to the crossroads where promise of immortality awaited.

With death as his final destination, his moral compass spinning wildly, his pockets full of useless proverbs, meaningless mantras and outworn parables he ran, ran toward the light. Besieged and betrayed by the hegemon and the flail, the whipping post and the grove, he ran into the night and disappeared in the dry, swirling dust of everlasting oneness on the bald mountain.

The Essence

You will find me in the hedgerows among the briars and wild honeysuckle, safely hidden in the places where people seldom go. In the gnarled, knotted branches of the birches and oaks, covered by the vibrant, green leaves, I rest. Just above the surface of the water I hover with the twin winged dragonfly and the swooping summer swallow. I leap the rocky waterfalls with the salmon as they return home and I nest down in the bower with the linnet and the bittern, singing the songs of life full throated and majestic. I ride on the winds that sweep across the dry, desert sands, and I roam with the nomads crisscrossing the vast, open tundra. I sway and caress the grasses that wave on the prairie and I dance and swirl among the leaves in the lush rainforest. I run with the wild horses across the wide-open plains and I soar with the eagle above the high mountain tops. I migrate with the herds, moving as one, along the time worn trails across the vast savannah and rest with them at night beside the watering holes. I shelter down in the sacred canyons and weave in and out of the dark, dusty passages and underground caverns. I swim the oceans on a never-ending journey with the creatures of the deep and I fall silently with the snows that blanket the poles.

The Survivor

On a cold, stark night in August 1588, as a fierce gale subsided and the clouds slowly parted, light from a full autumn moon revealed a horrific scene strewn along the shoreline. The drowned corpses of 800 doomed sailors, washed up by the raging Atlantic Ocean waves, lay scattered among the rocks and sand; the bodies, already stripped of all items of value, were left as carrion for packs of starving wild dogs and flocks of hungry ravens.
Broken chests full of gold, silver and jewels, were looted and carried off by bands of scavenging, local inhabitants. Concealed among the rushes, a short distance from the shore, a lone survivor, woken by the sounds of the feeding frenzy, wondered if he was having a horrible dream. Struggling upright, he propped himself on one elbow and let his gaze slowly wander the length of the strand, revealing the scene of utter carnage.

As his terrified mind raced and tried to make sense of the awful sight before him, memories started to return, and images of earlier events began to unfold. He remembered three ships fleeing in panic, a dangerously rocky shoreline, terrified fellow sailors, a violent storm and then... darkness.

Worms

A round, rusted tin can, contents long ago devoured, sat in patient
silence on the sloped window sill. The long-necked spade lounged
like a bored corner-boy, against the kitchen wall, waiting. Hickory
handle, time shaped by the grip of calloused hands, stained with the
spit of generations. The blade, honed with a degree of perfect
angle, ready to slice deep in the dark loam and uncover the life
beneath the surface. Foot planted firmly on the lug, driven deep,
sod turned, sharp tap with the back of the blade revealed
earthworms, black-heads and from under the roots of the dock, the
trout's favorite, fat, white grubs. Layer of soil in the can, a bed for
the worms, where squirming equality reigns.

The Potters Field

Deep in the thick clay that the potters once used, they lie. They lie forgotten and alone, outside the walled city in a field bought with the traitor's silver: their final stop on the long, torturous road to peace and salvation. Ignored in life and cast aside in death, they languish in the place where nothing grows, in deathly quietude, unknown, unwanted and a shame on the façade of glowing pretention and blissful, ignorant falsehood. Nameless, they lie, condemned in the shadow of the grove and the cold, dark place of the skulls.

City of Lights

The lights are dimmed in the city one more time.
Darkness, dark shadows, dark streets, dark mindlessness. It's wake
bathes all in black, forlorn in desperation. They wander, silent,
down the avenues and boulevards. Food uneaten, music unheard,
the game un-finished. Through the gardens, along the river, under
the bridges.

And the bells are cracked and silent. The ringed tower, begs for
mercy, yet stands triumphant. Tortured voices from Lachaise cry,
'no more, no more.' Blood and tears on the Rue, flow crimson,
then congeals in the cold night air, beneath a November sky, in the
City of Lights.

In my Blood

Tell me, what do you want from me?
What more can I give you?
Have I not given you enough?
Must I bleed all over the page
and purge my soul for all to see?
Rend open wide the deep dark rage,
will I then regain my sanity?
The mind in a whirl and racing
like a heartbeat bursting free.
Expel the thoughts, pain embracing
when once a story comes to be.
Can these words fulfill your need?
uncoil the depths of disparity.
Or bind you fast on endless seas
with roiling thoughts and fantasy.
Alas, blood must spill across the page
or else coagulation rules.
If not expressed, this hidden rage
will blind and smite us all as fools.
Once heart's blood has poured clear through
relief will come, and pain abate.
Released from fear if what I do,
is tell the tale with honest faith?
Tell me, is this what you want?
Is this enough? Tell me.

Ask not Why

Ask not why those shots rang out, their retort echoing across the crowded Plaza. Ask not why those bullets coursed through the warm Texan air, to strike with measured, deadly precision. Ask not why the smell of cordite invaded the senses and stung the innocent eyes. Ask not why the dreamers are always besieged by those who would conspire in the shadows. Ask not why their urge to drown potential in the abyss of negative thought, word and deadly deed.

Ask not why the inner light is detested and feared by the forces of darkness. Ask not why the lesser men are loosed in time to hate all, to undo what was almost complete. Ask not why the lamb was slaughtered in the arena by the ungodly, his blood congealed in the sawdust.

Ask not why the faceless brood bayed with savage, inhuman lust for his life force. Ask not why the contorted, brutish minds attempt to justify their twisted tenets. Ask not why evil holds its sway in a vise like grip with the tenacity of the hellish beast.

Instead ask how. How do we ensure that it does not repeat? How can we keep his message of hope and optimism alive? Ask what. What can we do for our country, our world? Ask when. When will we see the likes of him again? Ask where. Where do we begin? Remember, lest we forget the greatness stolen from us that bleak November day.

Freedom from Fear

The massive blasts of four homemade, two-hundred-pound mortars, launched from the rear of a commandeered, flatbed truck, reverberated and shook the buildings throughout the town as they hit their target with deadly precision. The night sky was set aglow with eerily brilliant domes of light as each shell exploded; the windowpanes in the houses closest to the target disintegrated into glinting shards, propelled hundreds of feet into the air by the huge shockwaves, deadly fingers of death for anyone unfortunate enough to be caught in their path. Roof slates cracked, loosened, and slid to the ground, laying shattered in broken piles in the street. Jagged, grotesquely twisted metal chunks of a Wessex helicopter, blown to pieces as it sat on its landing pad, whizzed through the night sky, landing in dozens of locations, some as far away as the cemetery, five hundred yards distant.

Heavy, rattling M60 machine-gun fire opened up from several vantage points, the armor-piercing tracer bullets glowing, as they coursed through the night air toward the British army barracks, striking, then ripping through the barrier walls. Automatic rifles sprayed the large observation post on the Square, ensuring those inside stayed there. In less than ten minutes, it was over. A hushed silence enveloped the town; all was quiet and still. The troops inside the joint Army/Police base did not venture outside for several hours. By then the volunteers had merged back into the Irish night and were long gone. This was life in my hometown for almost thirty years.

The Fox the Bird and the Poets

In the age when the Maigue, flowing broad from the Shannon, winding slow through the sloping place of Crom Dubh, right there, right on that spot, it all changed forever. For it was there that the long-ships carrying the sons of Thor along its' looped course, stopped below the fastness sited high above the grassed banks, and sent the Linnet skyward from the heather, in frightful flight. And it was there, right on that spot, where O'Donovan parleyed, swore fealty and ruled in safety with the invasive Dane. And it was there that O'Connor encircled the ramparts at Rathmore, burned the enclosures and routed the pretenders.

And it was there that the Norman puppet masters, with their Welsh and Flemish bowmen in tow, installed the Geraldines to rule in lieu. And it was there that Red Hugh, after the night time march across the frozen bogs, en-route to meet the Spaniard, met first with the Countess from Kildare. And it was there too that the hedge masters of Kilmallock gathered and birthed the written and spoken native tongue. Thus it was that the Fil Na Maigue rhyme was infused with life's breath and it was then, right then, on that very spot, in that very place, that the Limerick was born.

The Night Owls

I went down to the cool, dark woods,
when night owls were on the wing.
On earthly ghosts and raging floods
embraced my lonely pondering.
Moss clung fast to an olden tree,
near bank of river flowing slow.
Salmon leap I smiled to see,
in silence, with a young moons' glow.
Fawn eyes bright, shone out at me,
from in the depths, and to and fro.
She licked my hand, while nestling free,
her tale to tell of the long ago.
She told to me, through cool night air
that time and space are here and now.
Spoke to me of a maid so fair,
with haunted look on her pale brow.
An apple blossom in her hair,
she haunts the woods in search of him.
To heal her heart and her love fair,
and cease the lonely wanderin'.
All at once near a white oak tree,
a girl in shimmering bright light,
came out and gently called to me.
Then both did meld, into the night.

The Poet

If you were one of the inquisitive onlookers in Dublin on a remarkable day in April 1916, and if you were close enough, you couldn't fail to see the lone figure, silhouetted by the light of the still raging pyre that was once the splendid edifice, the General Post Office. There, between two of the large, bullet shattered, Ionic columns that supported the Greco/Roman pediment above the entrance, his broad brimmed fedora set at an angle over his brow, his greatcoat, dusty, torn, and bloodstained, stood a poet. You would be forgiven if you were not aware that the poet was about to complete his final stanza and immortalize a centuries old dream. If you looked closer still you would have been struck by the fact that although gaunt, disheveled, and shell-shocked, the poet's eyes still shone with the fierce brilliance of determination.

Adjusting his hat, and straightening his holster, he looked across the rubble strewn street and focused on the imposing figure of the Admiral, high atop the tall, granite pillar. 'Ah. Horatio, I fear I'll be joining you soon.' Then turning, he let his gaze linger for the last time, on the bronze, sculpted figure that stood at their command post in the center of the building. The sculpture, of the ancient warrior, Cu Chulainn, was one of the poet's mythical Irish heroes and source of inspiration. Cu Chulainn, depicted tied to a pillar, at his own request, is slumped in mortal agony, his head hung in glorious defeat, the shield falling from his grasp, yet still, his sword is clutched tightly in his right hand. A raven, with talons gripping the flesh on his shoulder, mirrored the poets deepening sense of foreboding.

'The hounds have cornered me too, Setanta.'

Turning toward the street once more, he scanned the faces of the assembled throng. How many of them will remember? Will they one day understand that we did it for them? Or will they simply forget? Then began the lonely walk to the barricade at Moore Street, nurse O'Farrell in step. Angry locals, some of whom he knew in his other life as a teacher and barrister, threw stones, spat at him and taunted him with shouts of, "Bloody rebel. Traitor. Fenian bastard. Shoot him. Shoot them all." The soldiers forming the cordon, their bayonets fixed, stared at him with unbridled, snarling contempt. He waited calmly for the uproar to subside, then, when it was silent, the poet stepped forward, removed his Sam Browne belt and holster and handed them to the British officer.

If you happened to be there six days earlier, on Easter Monday, you would have observed the same poet standing on the same spot, the marble columns, gleaming in the noonday sun, forming a perfect frame around him. You would have seen that his uniform was clean and neatly pressed the night before. His long greatcoat, with the sunlight reflecting off the two rows of brass buttons, dazzled the spectators, and forced those nearest him to shade their eyes. His revolver, holstered on a broad belt around his slim waist, was loaded and tested. You would have been mesmerized by the look in his eyes as they flashed with fervor in the knowledge that he was about to make history.

In his right hand he held a rolled-up parchment, his nation's destiny. Stepping forward, he opened the document and began to read. If you were still there and listened, really listened, you would have been awed by the poet's passion and conviction. The poet's name was Patrick Henry Pearse and what he dared to read was the "Proclamation of the Irish Republic." At four minutes past noon on Easter Monday 1916, in a steady, forceful voice, and calling on his ancestors for courage and strength, he proclaimed, once, and for all time, freedom for his country and its people. And thus it began, and the terrible beauty was born...

The Dublin General Post Office

Full Circle

From up here I watched as the harsh foreigner ousted the O'Neill, sacked his church and razed his castle. I shivered as a blinding snowstorm swirled through the valley of Mullaghbawn, swept over the brae and buried the kilns at Lislea. I called out to the Bard and the Bishops as they ran for their lives through the old slate quarry, seeking shelter from the royal henchmen, in the Doctor's quarters.

But from up here I have also seen enemy and foe alike come together, on common ground with hopeful intent of a peaceful dawn. My heart of granite, softened with words and gestures of a deeper courage and spirit, waits for it to come to pass. I have seen it all from up here. I am Gullion, and through it all, I have watched them come and go and still I remain unmoved, unbowed and unbroken, for I am Gullion, the mountain of steep slopes.

I see it all from up here.

ABOUT THE AUTHOR

Author John Anthony Brennan comes from Crossmaglen, a small tough town in County Armagh, Ireland. A town like Ireland herself, which has endured and survived through the centuries, despite the influence of the invaders' harsh heel. He left his beloved, sacred green isle many years ago to explore the world and has been island hopping ever since.

 He has traveled extensively, visiting many of the sacred sites and incorporates his experiences in both his prose and poetry as he believes that a common thread connects us all. He has previously written a philosophical memoir; a collection of memoir style poetry and a book on the history of Ireland. His latest production, "In the Realm of Spirit" is a collection of poems that captures the essence of the seen and unseen world around us.

His first book titled, "Don't Die with Regrets," written to inspire others to always follow their dreams, won the prestigious 2015 "Next Generation Indie Book" award in the Memoir category.

https://www.amazon.com/author/johnabrennan

Works by John A. Brennan

Don't Die with Regrets: Ireland and the Lessons My Father Taught Me

The Journey: A Nomad Reflects

Turn Out the Light

Out of the Ice: Ireland Then and Now

In the Realm of Spirit: Psalms From a Mountain

CPSIA information can be obtained
at www.ICGtesting.com
Printed in the USA
LVHW091731011118
595633LV00002B/237/P